THE ROSICRUCIAN EMBLEMS

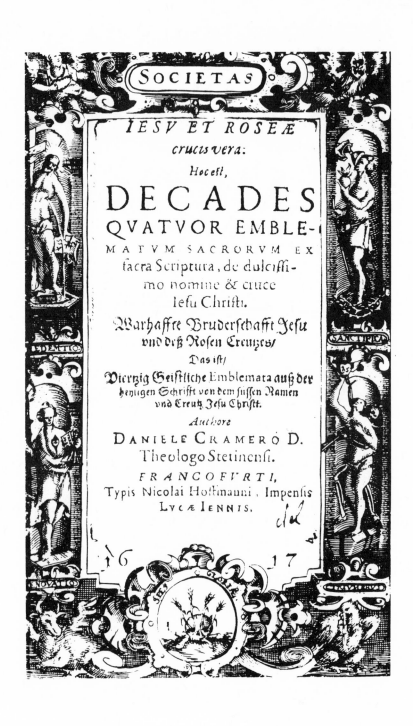

SOCIETAS

IESV ET ROSEÆ
crucis vera:

Hoc est,

DECADES
QVATVOR EMBLE-
MATVM SACRORVM EX
facra Scriptura, de dulciffi-
mo nomine & cruce
Iefu Chrifti.

Warhaffte Bruderschafft Jefu
vnd drß Rofen Creutzes/
Das ist/
Vierzig Geistliche Emblemata auß der
heiligen Schrifft von dem süssen Namen
vnd Creutz Jefu Chrifti.

Authore
DANIELE CRAMERO D.
Theologo Stetinensi.

FRANCOFVRTI,
Typis Nicolai Hoffmanni, Impensis
LVCÆ IENNIS.

16   17

THE ROSICRUCIAN EMBLEMS OF DANIEL CRAMER

THE TRUE SOCIETY OF JESUS AND THE ROSY CROSS

Here are forty sacred emblems from
Holy Scripture concerning
the most precious name and cross
of Jesus Christ

By Daniel Cramer

Master of Theology of Stettin

TRANSLATED FROM THE LATIN
BY FIONA TAIT

INTRODUCTION AND COMMENTARY
BY ADAM MCLEAN

MAGNUM OPUS HERMETIC SOURCEWORKS #4

PHANES PRESS
1991

This work, part of the Magnum Opus Hermetic Sourceworks series, was previously published in a handbound edition, limited to 250 copies, in 1980. The Magnum Opus Hermetic Sourceworks series is published under the General Editorship of Adam McLean.

Translation © 1991 by Fiona Tait
Introduction and Commentary © 1991 by Adam McLean

98 97 96 95 94 93 92 91   5 4 3 2 1

Published by Phanes Press, PO Box 6114, Grand Rapids, MI 49516, USA.

Library of Congress Cataloging-in-Publication Data

Cramer, Daniel
    [Societas Jesus et Rosae Crucis Vera. English]
    The Rosicrucian emblems of Daniel Cramer : the True Society of Jesus and the Rosy Cross : here are forty sacred emblems from Holy Scripture concerning the most precious name and cross of Jesus Christ / by Daniel Cramer ; translated from the Latin by Fiona Tait ; introduction and commentary by Adam McLean.
       p.   cm.
    Translation of: Societas Jesus et Rosae Crucis Vera.
    ISBN 0-933999-87-9 (alk. paper) — ISBN 0-933999-88-7 (pbk. : alk. paper)
    1. Rosicrucians—Prayer-books and devotions—English—Early works to 1800. 2. Christian art and symbolism—Early works to 1800. 3. Emblems—Early works to 1800. 4. Hermetism—Early works to 1800. 5. Society of Rosicrucians. I. McLean, Adam. II. Title. III. Series: Magnum Opus Hermetic Sourceworks (Series) ; no. 4.
BF1623.R7C78813   1991
135'.43—dc20   90-47420
                                                                               CIP

This book is printed on alkaline paper which conforms to the permanent paper standard developed by the National Information Standards Organization.

Printed and bound in the United States

Contents

Introduction

This almost unknown work by Daniel Cramer of his 40 sacred emblems should be recognized as a Rosicrucian item of great interest. This very rare book was published in 1617 at the height of the Rosicrucian publishing period, and only a year after the appearance of the *Chemical Wedding of Christian Rosencreutz*. Cramer received a short mention in A. E. Waite's *Brotherhood of the Rosy Cross*, London, 1924, p. 234:

> In 1616 Daniel Cramer, a Protestant theologian who taught at Wittenburg and Stettin, produced a tract entitled *Societas Jesus et Rosae Crucis Vera*.

Little is known of Cramer, but it seems that he was, as Waite suggests, a Protestant theologian, and published various works between 1595 and 1620 including *Orations on the Most Sweet Name of Jesus*, a work *In Memory of the Birth of Martin Luther*, an essay "Against the Jesuits," *The Reward through Grace*, and other books of a theological nature.

In addition to the heading of the title page in *The True Society of Jesus and the Rosy Cross*, there are also a number of internal Rosicrucian references relating the symbols of the rose, the heart, and the cross (in particular see Emblems 19, 22, and 31). *The True Society of Jesus* obviously has no direct connection with the Jesuits, the 'Society of Jesus' of St. Ignatius of Loyola, as Cramer's other writings show him to be a strong Lutheran Protestant. Indeed, one of his essays was entitled "Against the Jesuits." However, perhaps we can recognize a parallel between these emblems and the Spiritual Exercises of St. Ignatius of Loyola; it is quite possible that here Cramer was consciously trying to produce a series of spiritual exercises of a Protestant esoteric Christianity.

A further Rosicrucian connection is made through the publisher, Luca Jennis of Frankfurt. Jennis, who was connected with the well-known Rosicrucian publisher Theodorus de Bry, published many of the works of Michael Maier, Daniel Mylius, and other alchemical writers, and seems to have been particularly interested in publishing works using emblematic figures.

Early in the unfolding of Rosicrucian esotericism, a particular impulse arose for the ideas to be conveyed through symbols, and especially through long series of integrated symbols in the form of emblematic plates. The student had to work these symbols into his being through meditation so that he could grasp the whole series as a totality, seeing the various interrelationships between the different emblems and inwardly experiencing the process of the development of the symbols unfolded through the sequence. This was one of the ways in which the Rosicrucians revealed and yet kept secret their esotericism.

The Forty Sacred Emblems stands completely in contrast to Cramer's other writings. This series of 40 emblematic plates, each bearing a title together with a verse from the Bible and two lines in Latin, is especially connected with the heart. Cramer provided an extended meditative exercise of an esoteric Christianity based on the symbol of the heart. The heart, which is found in nearly all the plates, undergoes various processes and experiences through this cycle of 40 stages.

Thus we can see here an extended meditative Rosicrucian exercise working upon the heart-center of Man. In the Eastern Tantric tradition, the various centers of etheric forces within the body of Man were pictured as chakras or lotus flowers with various numbers of petals. The yogi meditated upon symbols and feelings associated with each of the petals of a particular chakra and thus gained awareness of the conscious use of these centers within Man's subtle body. We have here, in the Cramer Emblems, a Western parallel in this series of Rosicrucian meditative exercises that also open up the meditator to consciousness of the heart-center. These heart meditations also reveal the esoteric Christianity, which was the cornerstone of the Rosicrucian Mystery stream, for the Rosicrucians brought into the Western mystical tradition a definite current of esoteric Christianity. Thus we should see the Cramer Emblems as an important work, revealing an aspect of Rosicrucianism not always clearly perceived by commentators on the tradition.

The symbolism found in the 40 emblems is to some extent alchemical. In some plates we see the heart being placed in a furnace, in others it is weighed in a balance, at one stage various plant forms grow from its substance, and in others it is set free from various types of bondage and limitation.

These illustrations are very simple and communicate directly to the soul in contrast to many other series of emblems from the same period, which are often obscure and enigmatic and require a key to penetrate their mystery. The Cramer Emblems are a most approachable symbol system and it seems likely that this was intended as a popular book that would appeal to a wide audience, as the symbols are so archetypal and straightforward.

Perhaps we might draw a parallel between Daniel Cramer and another Protestant theologian, Johann Valentine Andreae, who is credited with writing the *Chemical Wedding of Christian Rosencreutz*. Both of these figures wrote ponderous theological tomes in the best Lutheran Protestant tradition, both were in some way drawn into the Rosicrucian movement, and both produced a particular piece of writing which stands in total contrast to their other works and which sought to popularize Rosicrucian esoteric philosophy—Cramer with his most approachable Emblems, and Andreae with his entertaining story of the Chemical Wedding.

—ADAM MCLEAN

To the highest and most illustrious
Prince and Lord
Philip II
Duke of Stettin, of the Pomeranians, Cassubans and the Vandals
Prince of Rugen, Count of Gutzonia, Ruler of the Provinces of
Lwow and Butow
To his most merciful Lord

Most high and illustrious wise Prince,

No one can be unaware of the great value placed upon the pictorial art by antiquity, unless he is clearly a stranger to reading the historians. For Pliny tells us (Book 35, Chapter I) that this art was once sought out for Kings and peoples, for the sake of those whom they thought worthy of being handed down in memory to posterity. Pliny also says that such great honor was accorded it, that nobles practiced it, and soon honorable men were taught it, not slaves, though this had always been forbidden. It is because of this art that Apelles hovers on men's lips, and

Everlasting fame, on a wing that cannot tire, drives him on.

Who is there who does not know how pleasing this art has been, and still is, to Princes of our age? It is a joy, a most delightful and sweet exercise by men of talent. Who would [not] contemplate the medley of emblems represented by this art and consecrated to posterity, pleasing and skillful, by Jupiter!, as many outstanding men have employed their genius in this matter. For—to say nothing of the hieroglyphic signs of the Egyptians, by which they depicted their wishes and intentions—who does not wonder at and revere the labours of Alciati, Reusner and Claudius Pardinus on this study? Who does not perceive the certain, singular delight in them, while the learning is abstruse, concealed and hidden in them, like the fellow in the Comic poet, who contemplated she who reposed within the wax?

Pursuing the tracks of these men, the Reverend and most noble Master Daniel Cramer, S.S. Doctor of Theology, has shown the brilliance of his genius, although in a different subject, so far not touched upon by the rest, that is, a holy subject; and he has handed to me these emblems, which ought to be cut in copper and committed to the light. Just as he has a singular zeal and desire in putting forward these studies, so have I joyfully taken this work upon me. For I am persuaded that by new example he has gained all applause in this subject, not just because he mixes the useful with the pleasing, but because he has taken it from the pure streams of Israel.

Deservedly then, most high Prince, I have wished, and it is my duty, to dedicate all this work to your Highness, both because Master Cramer's bud of genius has been nourished and protected by the sun and splendor of none other but your Highness, and it seems not unreasonable to me it should wish to revisit its natural shores; and also, because I know these skillful exercises find favor with your Highness, and it has always been a particular specialty, as it were, of the Dukes of Pomerania, never to desist from promoting the arts and the cultivators of them.

Therefore your Highness receives this small gift with pleasure, especially for the sake of the Reverend Cramer; and since I have no incense, let him permit me to propriate with salt-cakes, and may the breath of your favor think it not unworthy to breathe on me, and my studies.

With this, I commend your Highness, together with your most illustrious family, to God, thrice-greatest, to thrive most happily, live long, and prosper to eternity.

From the Academy of Giessen,
the eleventh of March, 1617.

Your serene Highness' most humble servant;

James Muller of Torgau.

TO THE READER

The fruit for us indeed is in our most holy Bible. The pagans thought that only in their own heathen writers existed emblems, mottoes, illustrated maxims, hieroglyphs. Correct then this opinion. Act so you may show that our field is not sterile. Rather reproach yourself at the negligence of the world, which cares less for the reading of the Bible than the writings of the Gentiles. If this my SOCIETY has achieved anything towards checking this error, I shall congratulate myself. I shall rejoice for you. Farewell, Christian reader, and if you are a Christian, take diligent care to read the Bible.

From the Academy at Stettin
the month of August, 1616.

D.C.D.

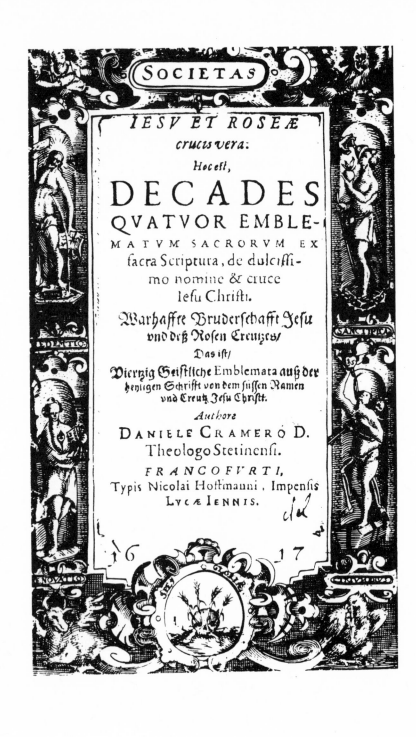

SOCIETAS

IESV ET ROSEÆ
crucis vera:
Hoc est,

DECADES
QVATVOR EMBLE-
MATVM SACRORVM EX
facra Scriptura, de dulciffi-
mo nomine & cruce
Iefu Chrifti.

Warhaffte Bruderfchafft Jefu
vnd dɾß Rofen Creutzes/
Das ift/
Viertzig Geiftliche Emblemata auß der
heiligen Schrifft von dem füffen Namen
vnd Creutz Jefu Chrift.
Authore
DANIELE CRAMERO D.
Theologo Stetinenfi.

FRANCOFVRTI,
Typis Nicolai Hoffmanni, Impenfis
LVCÆ IENNIS.

1 6   1 7

Frontispiece Prefatory to the Emblems of this Book Devised and Cut in Copper by the Most Learned and Skilled Master James Muller

The Spirit that creates poetry moves within those
Who show weighty matters represented in pictures
For what is a picture, but a silent poem?
The name of each applies to both.
And who would deny to a painter what is allowed
Under the old law, to a poet?
You may here, with your first look, gaze on the emblems of the
   book;
The sculpted image teaches which are good, and which devout.

REDEMPTION

The fount of life, from whose bubbling spring full rivers flow,
Shows itself in the first shadow of a picture.
It is your bond, Sinner, destroyed on the Cross,
Which this flow from the blood of Christ quenches.
Since the Cross and the wave of salvation
Destroy your rich debt of sin, you will be redeemed.

RENEWAL

After, redeemed by the blood of Christ, you will be joyful,
And will busy yourself to know rightly the Word of God.
This Spirit will be a light to you, by its shining
You will truly know the heavenly commandments of God.
You will not fear the law, nor the anger and thunder of the law,
For the very favor of the Gospel blesses you.

SANCTIFICATION

Now that you have known Christ, by the shining lamp of
    heaven,
There has arisen in you thirst for the Good.
The heavenly cup refreshes you, so all desire
Within your heart drains away and perishes.
So, Sinner, do you still fear the thorns of the world?
You can go safely on the cruel thorns.

TRIUMPH

Full grace has received you into the number of the holy.
How suddenly does cruel death lay snares for you?
See, it attacks openly, pierces you with sharp spear.
But the heart strives to reach the heavenly home,
Though bright death stretches forth its consuming hand at it,
The heart, triumphing, overcomes in the name of Jesus.

HOPE OF GLORY

At last the Corpse-Goddess has covered your body and head,
Buried in the grave beneath the tomb,
And there exists on earth nothing more
Of what was you or your possessions.
Hope of life conquers when the dead flesh rises again,
As corn grows strong when brought to life.

And so, Reader, you have the work of death and life,
The embossings of the Holy page, and a short epigram.
These will be able to show and teach your mind
What your state was once and what it may become today.
You had been guilty of sin: Christ purifies all guilt
By the fount from his own side.

The Spirit illuminates all corners of the heart,
And renews you through the Gospel.
The heavenly drink calms the ferment of the heart,
Thus fortified you pass beyond the bloody weapons.
Death lays snares for the heart inscribed with the name of Jesus,
But, unharmed, it seeks the kingdoms of the sky.
Certain hope of heavenly salvation remains,
When new warmth frees the resurrected bones.
Do not doubt: all this is proved twice over;
Do you not see the proofs? Every angel has them.
The skillful craft of Muller has set out all these things,
Dear Reader, and given you them for viewing.
Why are you now amazed at the sculptings of Phidias' chisel?
To Muller rather than to Phidias, heaven comes.

To the most excellent and learned
Master James Muller L.L.
studious companion and dearest friend

You who marvel at the hand of Phidias, the brush of Appelles
The genius and skill of Zeuxis,
And others distinguished from the crowd,
Whose famous names, cherishing antiquity has inscribed with
    immortality,
Cease to wonder: it was relentless work raised them,
And caused them to hum upon the learned lips of men.
Let those who have superseded vain application and drudgery,
Press the former underfoot.
See, they show us a new example; inimitable by none,
Desired by many; emblems engraved for you.
These Muller has chiseled with judgment,
Taking only a little time, while he follows the allurement of
    genius,
To each, others have attributed an age,
To Muller but a few hours, yet his art is no less.
What they have done was by study, play and labor;
He, by an almost innate gift, has created this delight.

Geissen,

Christopher Witke
Saltquellensis

The Rosicrucian Emblems

The teaching of the Lord crowns.

I know nothing, I am capable of nothing, I am nothing;
The fact that by my face and nature,
I am seen to partake of these three,
Is all due to God.

FIRST DECADE

Emblem 1

I GROW SOFT

"Is not my word . . . like a hammer that breaks the rock
in pieces." (Jeremiah 23:29)

My heart is like a rock, the hammer softens me,
I sustain the blow; why then, if only I might be better.

Emblem 2

I INCREASE

"But that on the good ground are they, which in an honest and good heart, having heard the word, keep it and bring forth fruit with patience." (Luke 8:15)

I am not a road, or a thorn, or a stone, but the best earth;
And sweet ears of corn will rise from the bosom of my heart.

Emblem 3

I SEEK THE HEIGHTS

"Deliver me, O Lord, from mine enemies, I flee unto thee
to hide me." (Psalms 143:9)

I flee to you, Jesus, since the enemy seeks me;
Seize my heart as spoil, lest I am taken as plunder.

Emblem 4

I LOVE

"Blow upon my garden, that the spices thereof may flow out."
(Song of Solomon 4:16)

Let me be kindled, Jesus, by your incense and breath;
I flame, let yours be the love; I am fragrant,
let yours be the scent.

Emblem 5

I AM CONCEALED

"That thou wouldst keep me secret until thy wrath be spent."
(Job 14:13)

He is as a shield to me, until anger passes over;
It is he who reconciles himself to me, me to him.

Emblem 6

I AM ILLUMINATED

"In thy light shall we see light." (Psalms 36:9)

I see the light in your light, let darkness be far away,
He is wise who gains wisdom from the book of the Lord.

Emblem 7

I AM CONSTANT

"My heart was hot within me, while I was musing
the fire burned." (Psalms 39:3)

Blow winds, I meditate, by contemplation am I fired on the altar,
The more I am stirred, the hotter I become.

Emblem 8

I BREATHE

"For we are unto God a sweet savour of Christ."
(2 Corinthians 2:15)

My heart is redolent with the incense of prayers,
Since the sweet smelling force of God renews me;
Hence we are smoke and fair fragrance.

Emblem 9

I AM FREED

"... forgetting those things which are behind, and reaching forth unto those things which are before." (Philippians 3:13)

The world wants me for itself; Jesus who freed me wants me:
The former is the world's jealousy, the latter is His love.

Emblem 10

I COME ALIVE AGAIN

"And the light shineth in darkness." (John 1:5)

Should he, to whom Jesus is the light, the life,
To whom He gives light and warmth in heaven,
fear even death when he dies?

SECOND DECADE

Emblem 11

I LIVE

"For to me, to live is Christ and to die is gain."
(Philippians 1:21)

Christ is life for me, complete life,
Death's ceremony will be my profit, not the end.

Emblem 12

I AM HEALED

"For he hath torn, and he will heal us." (Hosea 6:1)

When he burns, he cures; he heals, when he wounds;
He anoints when he pierces;
He cuts, but he does not kill with the sword.

Emblem 13

I AM ENDANGERED

"Deep calleth unto deep at the noise of the water spouts."
(Psalms 42:7)

The wave tosses, the storm exults, and the rain pours down,
But the shell of hope lightens the heart of every trouble.

Emblem 14

I AM CRUCIFIED

"I am crucified with Christ, nevertheless I live: yet not I, but
Christ liveth in me." (Galatians 2:19)

I live, indeed, my life and sighs are directed upward:
How often, Christ, am I pierced on your cross.

Emblem 15

I MEDITATE

"As we have therefore opportunity, let us do good unto all men." (Galatians 6:9)

The centuries fly by, the days pass away,
Every man must work for the good, while there is an hour of time.

Emblem 16

I AM REDEEMED

"If riches increase, set not your heart upon them."
(Psalms 62:10)

Even the things which pass away often bind and capture the
heart. Take the key from the Lord, you will be free.

Emblem 17

I BECOME SWEET

"To the one we are the savour of death unto death, and to the other the savour of life unto life." (2 Corinthians 2:16)

The cross, the bitterness, the smell of Christ are deadly to others, but to me they are life, the cross is love and sweet scent.

Emblem 18

I AM NOTHING

"For we know that the law is spiritual, but I am carnal."
(Romans 7:14)

I am nothing, but I am lightened by the Gospel and am triumphant. Thus grace prevails over the law, I seek the stars.

Emblem 19

I OUTWEIGH

"For ye are not under the law, but under grace."
(Romans 6:14)

The heart, stained on the rosy altar of Christ's blood,
Overcomes the weight of the law by the triumphing
weight of the cross.

Emblem 20

I BUILD MYSELF UP

"A wise man which built his house upon a rock."
(Matthew 7:24)

Christ is a rock for me, hope and a pillar of safety,
Upon which I am built, while the wave of Styx rages.

THIRD DECADE

Emblem 21

I AM ABSOLVED

"(Christ) . . . having forgiven you all trespasses, blotting out the handwriting of ordinances that was against us which was contrary to us . . ." (Colossians 2:14)

A great lawsuit has been brought against me;
Only the golden cross of Christ has given satisfaction,
only it will satisfy.

Emblem 22

I AM NOT WOUNDED

"As the lily among thorns . . ." (Song of Solomon 2:2)

Here we are among thorns, among shingles, troubles;
Yet with the rosy flower, our lilies thrive.

Emblem 23

I AM PREDESTINED

"And another shall call himself by the name of Jacob, and another shall subscribe with his hand unto the Lord."
(Isaiah 44:5)

I am numbered among those of Christ, by whose name I am known. He is the title, the quill, the book of my life.

Emblem 24

I AM TRIED IN THE FIRE

"I have chosen thee in the furnace of affliction." (Isaiah 4:10)

The Lord burns and tries us in the fire of the furnace.
May you be upright and constant, and you will be proved good.

Emblem 25

I AM COOLED

"For I will pour water upon him that is thirsty, and floods upon the dry ground, I will pour my spirit upon thy seed." (Isaiah 44:3)

I burn and sweat in hardships,
But the kind spirit and the heavenly water are sweet coolants.

Emblem 26

I AM PROTECTED

"He that dwelleth in the secret place of the most High, shall abide under the shadow of the Almighty. I will say of the Lord, he is my refuge and my fortress." (Psalms 91:2)

What shall I fear?
The dense shadows from the wings of Jehovah enfold me,
Lest I should be boiled down by the fire of grim anger.

Emblem 27

I ENDURE MOCKERY

"Well is he that is defended from the tongue."
(Ecclesiastes 28:23)

My innocent heart is imprisoned by the encircling world.
Why should mockery or evil tongue harm me?

Emblem 28

I AM FAITHFUL

"Be thou faithful unto death and I will give thee a crown of life."
(Revelation 2:10)

Let the mind be trusting, let there be faith and concord,
Even unto the destruction of death,
And there will be, assuredly, a gilded door in the sky.

Emblem 29

I FEAR HELL

"For their worm shall not die, neither shall their fire
be quenched." (Isaiah 66:24)

The conscious mind feels wounds devoid of wicked rest,
So beware this eater of flesh, whoever you are.

Emblem 30

I HOPE FOR RENEWAL

"And the dove came in to him in the evening, and lo, in her mouth was an olive leaf plucked off." (Genesis 8:10)

Now evening comes, may the leaf-bearing bird come also,
And make an end of the world in flood.

FOURTH DECADE

Emblem 31

HE WHO IS THIRSTY WILL DRINK

"But the water that I shall give him shall be in him a well of
water springing up into everlasting life." (John 4:14)

The mouth is wet with the rosy liquor,
From which fount the thirsty heart gushes out;
Thence the rose bursts into bloom.

Emblem 32

DIRT: FILTH

"For where your treasure is, there will your heart be."
(Matthew 6:21)

The heart leaves the place it has reached,
For it is an exile in all this gold;
Call back the heart, go glorified and courageous to the sky.

Emblem 33

SUFFER AND LEARN

"The words of the Lord are pure words as silver tried in a furnace of earth, purified seven times." (Psalms 12:6)

The brick and hearth witness to the quality of gold;
The same may testify to the goodness of the mind.

Emblem 34

NEITHER ON THIS SIDE, NOR ON THE OTHER

". . . we will not turn to the right hand nor to the left."
(Numbers 20:17)

Not in this place, not in that;
The heart will go more safely in the middle.
He who rushes from the mean, runs to destruction.

Emblem 35

SIMPLE WISDOM

"Be ye therefore wise as serpents, and harmless as doves."
(Matthew 10:16)

He whose heart is saved by simplicity, whose eye by wisdom,
Will be both serpent and dove to God.

Emblem 36

O VANITY!

"This people . . . honoureth me with their lips, but their heart is far from me." (Matthew 15:8)

One spirit drives the mind and jaw, let mouth and heart speak:
Faith does not tolerate discordant lyres.

Emblem 37

I MUST LEAVE

"For here have we no continuing city, but we seek one to come." (Hebrews 13:14)

My home is away from home, this homeland is not my country.
I must go; I reject this, I hope for another.
I do not want a worthless Good.

Emblem 38

I SIGH

"Come unto me all ye that labor and are heavy laden, and I will give you rest." (Matthew 11:28)

I fail beneath the cross; the same cross renews me;
The hand which made me sick heals; why therefore do I delay?

Emblem 39

DEATH IS A PROFIT

"... having a desire to depart and be with Christ."
(Philippians 1:23)

This life is a prison, the punishment is the sentence of death,
The provisions and interest are death, the honour is horror.

Emblem 40

THUS I AM NOURISHED

"For wheresoever the carcase is, there will the eagles be gathered together." (Matthew 24:28)

Your eagle's heart and sight, my Christ, the corpse lives;
Where you have been, there shall I always be.

Commentary

by Adam McLean

By way of a commentary to this book, I would like to outline one particular interpretation or way of working with these emblems, which I believe will help to throw some light on their significance as a symbolic system illustrating a process of spiritual development. This commentary, however, is not intended as a complete statement of the content of these emblems, but should be seen as only one interpretation, one facet of approach to this series. As with other systems of Hermetic symbols, the Cramer Emblems are multi-dimensional, they allow many different ways of working with their symbols. Indeed, it was part of the training of the Hermetic student to work, in inner imaginative meditations, through various patterns of interpretation. The essence of the symbolist tradition in Hermeticism lay in the fact that it conveyed its message on many different levels, and communicated above the one dimensional world of the intellectual, analytical facet of consciousness.

With the proviso that the interpretation outlined here is merely one way of working with these emblems, I suggest that we begin by analytically breaking down the whole series into parts, then synthesizing these parts into a whole.

We note that the series breaks down naturally into twenty paired emblems that reflect and complement each other, both through their pictorial elements and also the meaning assigned to them. Two obvious examples are Emblem 18 (I am nothing) and Emblem 19 (I outweigh) in which we see a polarity. Most of the pairings are, likewise, quite obvious and straightforward, but a few are more subtle, such as Emblem 31 (He who is thirsty will drink) and Emblem 34 (Neither on this side nor on the other). Here the underlying element is the balancing of forces. In 31 we see the human figure drinking in the spiritual nourishment which he then gives out through his heart, and achieves a balance between the

receiving and the giving of spiritual forces. The balancing element
of 34 is more obvious pictorially. The complete set of these pairings
of the Emblems is as follows:

1 – 23		9 – 16		24 – 33	
2 – 22		10 – 11		27 – 36	
3 – 37		12 – 25		29 – 30	
4 – 8		13 – 20		31 – 34	
5 – 26		14 – 21		32 – 39	
6 – 15		17 – 35		38 – 40	
7 – 28		18 – 19			

Meditation on these pairs will give rise to an awareness of the
essential polarities in these symbols.

Next, after this analysis, we have to unite these pairs together
into larger units, and ultimately into a totality. We find that they
form quaternities united by a common element, either by an
obvious pictorial aspect or by a more inner connection, which
involves the meaning of these emblems. When these are followed
in a particular order we find that there is outlined a process of inner
spiritual development through a series of ten stages. The heart of
man undergoes, through this process of inner development, a series
of experiences that are pictured in these ten stages. The 'heart' here
refers to the indwelling spiritual self of Mankind, the spiritual core,
which finds its inner home in Man's soul being, in the heart-center,
the central chakra of the soul.

The readers should follow this interpretation in the same
manner as did the Hermetic students of earlier times, by working
these symbols into their inner imaginative world through meditative exercises so that they can easily call them up before their
inward eye.

The first stage is the awareness that the heart or spiritual self
must have of the EARTHLY SNARES, of its being bound to the limitations of the worldly realm. This we find pictured in the four
emblems of this stage—27 (I endure mockery) and 36 (O Vanity!);
32 (Dirt: Filth) and 39 (Death is a gain). Here the uniting concept is
conveyed in the meaning of the symbols rather than in a direct

pictorial manner. In this first stage, the heart of humanity is bound and limited, but will become conscious of these limitations.

In the second stage, the stage of ASPIRATION, the heart seeks to escape the limitations of the worldly realm. We see this expressed in Emblem 3 (I seek the heights) and Emblem 37 (I must leave), both of which show the heart flying and seeking a new realm. The other two emblems of this quaternity are 40 (Thus am I nourished), which shows the heart being nourished on the body of Christ (including the Christ heart) which bears the five wounds, and Emblem 38 (I sigh) indicates the soul of mankind being inspired to climb towards the cross shown within a heart-shaped radiance.

Then follows the INWARD DEVELOPMENT stage described by the quaternity of emblems—6 (I am illuminated) and 15 (I meditate); 1 (I am softened) and 23 (I am predestined). These describe inner experiences of the heart as the spiritual self of man sets out on the quest for his spiritual source. In Emblem 6, the eye in the heart signifies that the seeker has achieved a consciousness of the heart center, an illumination. He meditates, and we see in Emblem 15 the heart lying upon the altar of the self between an hourglass and a book, meditation requiring both time and a content, a substance for the meditation. In Emblem 1, the hand of the spirit beats the heart with a hammer and softens it, making it inwardly responsive to the illumination of the spirit, and in 23 the hand of the spirit inscribes the name of Jesus upon the heart of Man. We note that in all four of these emblems the heart rests upon a solid object: a book, altar, or anvil.

The being of Man having now made some development, a certain solidity or INNER FOUNDATION is established during the next stage. The pair of emblems 9 (I am freed) and 16 (I am redeemed) both show the heart being freed by the hand of the spirit from entanglement in the earthly realm. The other pair in this quaternity, Emblem 7 (I am constant) and Emblem 28 (I am faithful), have a fourfold solidity in their pictorial form. The heart-center here has achieved an inner foundation.

Then follows the stage of the WARMING of the heart-center through the pair 24, (I am tried in the fire) and 33 (To suffer is to learn), both showing the heart being placed in a furnace. Emblems

4 (I love) and 8 (I breathe) both reveal the hand of the spirit dropping a balm or incense upon the heart, which is placed over a fire. The inner warmth of the spirit is woven into the heart-center from without. This marks the fifth stage of the whole process, and this engendering of inner warmth brings to a close its first half.

The second half of the process opens with the sixth stage, that of the BALANCING OF OPPOSITES. The heart has so far experienced various polarities and now must bring these together as it achieves more awareness of its spiritual foundation. Thus the pair of emblems, 31 (He who is thirsty will drink) and 34 (Neither to one side nor to the other), incorporate this balancing as described earlier (note also that in Emblem 31 the stream of spirit flowing from the heart nourishes a rose, a further Rosicrucian reference). The other pair in this quaternity, Emblem 12 (I am healed) and Emblem 25 (I am cooled), also picture this balancing of polarities. In 12 we see the heart both wounded by the sword and healed by the balm from the hand of the spirit (and perhaps this illustration has some connection with Rosicrucian writer Robert Fludd's idea of the weapon salve). Similarly, in Emblem 25 the hand of the spirit pours a cooling libation on the heart which is being heated on a fire.

During the next stage of the process which we may call the GROWTH-DEVELOPMENT, we find in Emblems 2 (I increase) and 22 (I am not wounded) the heart lying in a nest of dead thorns; but new growth is sprouting through the heart. In 18 (I am nothing) the heart is overcome by the weight of the law of Moses, but in 19 (I outweigh), with the cross and chalice of the blood of Christ, it outweighs the old law. Inner development and growth can then occur.

The SHIELDING-PROTECTIVE stage follows in which the heart must be shielded from the external forces in order that its inner essence may unfold: thus 5 (I am shielded) and 26 (I am protected). The other pair shows the heart endangered by the storm and the watery element; thus in Emblem 13 (I am endangered), and in Emblem 20 (I build myself up) the heart has built itself up above the waves on a pillar, secure and safe from the storm.

In the CRUCIFIXION stage following, we see in Emblem 17 (I become sweet) the sweetening aspect of the Cross, with the bees making honey. In Emblem 35 (The simple wisdom) the Cross serves to array various symbols of the simple wisdom of the spirit. The heart consciousness on the one side is balanced with the head consciousness on the other limb of the Cross, represented by the eye. The Dove of peace within the soul balances the serpent rising from below. The other pair in this quaternity, Emblem 14 (I am crucified) and 21 (I am absolved), reflect two well-known aspects of this stage. The spiritual heart of Man undergoes at this stage of spiritual development an inner crucifixion.

The RESURRECTION or RENEWAL stage shows in Emblems 10 (I come alive again) and 11 (I live) the restoration to new life, the dead skull rising as the winged living heart. Emblems 29 (I fear Hell) and 30 (I hope for renewal) show two birds perching upon the heart, the Vulture of the infernal realm and the Dove of spiritual peace, which holds within its beak the new sprouting branch, and the allegory of Noah's flood is indicated by the appearance of the Ark upon a hill in the background.

We find in this series of emblems an integrated process of spiritual development taking place through ten stages, and we can also see that the process as outlined here has many parallels with the Alchemical process of inner development, and also with symbols familiar in Western mysticism. The interpretation outlined here represents only one way of working with these symbols and the reader will recognize connections between the emblems other than those focussed on here. A series such as this is capable of many levels of interpretation, and Hermetic students once worked to explore their inner world through meditative exercises based on emblems such as these. This series of emblems, in common with others produced during the early 17th century, are really maps of the inner world—tools for exploring the psyche—and as such they are subtle tools with many edges and facets, capable of multiple levels of interpretation.

17	35	10	11
CRUCIFIXION		RESURRECTION	
14	21	29	30
2	22	5	26
GROWTH-DEVELOPMENT		SHIELDING-PROTECTIVE	
18	19	13	20
24	33	31	34
WARMING		BALANCING OF OPPOSITES	
4	8	12	25
6	15	9	16
INWARD DEVELOPMENT		INNER FOUNDATION	
1	23	7	28
27	36	3	37
EARTHLY SNARES		ASPIRATION	
32	39	38	40

I hope that in putting this work into circulation again, people will be encouraged to work through into an inner awareness of the content of these symbols. They speak so directly to us, even some four centuries after they were created, that one feels convinced that the authors here touched upon an archetypal level, an eternal reality in the human soul, that makes their symbolism resonate and resound in our souls today. A work as profound and as simple as this can never die, but must always be a vital source of inspiration.

Magnum Opus Hermetic Sourceworks

The Magical Calendar
The Mosaical Philosophy - Cabala
The Crowning of Nature
The Rosicrucian Emblems of Cramer
The Hermetic Garden of Daniel Stolcius
The Rosary of the Philosophers
The Amphitheatre Engravings of Heinrich Khunrath
Splendor Solis
The 'Key' of Jacob Boehme
The Revelation of Revelations of Jane Leade
A Commentary on the Mutus Liber
The Steganographia of Trithemius
The Origin and Structure of the Cosmos
A Commentary on Goethe's Fairy Tale
A Treatise on Angel Magic
The Paradoxical Emblems of Freher
The Heptarchia Mystica of John Dee
The Chemical Wedding of Christian Rosenkreutz
Alchemical Engravings of Mylius
The Five Books of Mystical Exercises of John Dee
Atalanta Fugiens of Michael Maier
The Kabbalistic Diagrams of Rosenroth

In addition to issuing the Magnum Opus Hermetic Sourceworks series, PHANES PRESS both publishes and distributes many fine books which relate to the philosophical, religious and spiritual traditions of the Western world. To obtain a copy of our current catalogue, please write:

PHANES PRESS
PO BOX 6114
GRAND RAPIDS, MI 49516
USA